[GLOBAL NETWORK REALTY]

# How to Create Passive Income with Rental Property

**Becoming a Successful Landlord, Investor, Entrepreneur**

**Nancy Huff**
with
**Keith Huff**

Scripture quotations marked NIV are taken from the Holy Bible, New International Version®, NIV®. Copyright © 1973, 1978, 1984, 2011 by Biblica, Inc.®. All rights reserved worldwide.

14 13 12 11   10 9 8 7 6 5 4 3 2 1

*How to Create Passive Income with Rental Property: Becoming a Successful Landlord, Investor, Entrepreneur*
Copyright © 2013
by Nancy Huff with Keith Huff
All rights reserved. No part of this book may be reproduced in any form without permission in writing from the author. Reviewers may quote brief passages in reviews.
Published by Huff Squared Publishing
P. O. Box 700832, Tulsa, OK 74170

Printed in the United States of America

# Table of Contents

| | |
|---|---:|
| Introduction | 1 |
| Needed - Local Landlords | 3 |
| You Can Be a Great Landlord – and Make Money Too | 7 |
| Rule # 1: You Have a Business, Not a Hobby | 19 |
| Rule # 2: Separate Business and Personal Expense | 31 |
| Rule # 3: Select Good Tenants | 34 |
| Rule # 4: Make Timely Repairs | 42 |
| Rule # 5: Keep Rents and Repairs Separate | 46 |
| Rule # 6: Find Excellent, Dependable Contractors | 49 |
| Rule # 7: Know When to Transition to a Property Management Company | 52 |
| Rule # 8: Never Spend All Your Cash Flow | 56 |
| Rule # 9 Craft a Great Lease Agreement | 59 |
| Rule #10: Keep Count of Pets and Other Animals | 62 |
| Be a Socially Responsible Landlord | 66 |
| Sample Rental Fix-up and Repair Checklist | 78 |
| About the Authors | 84 |

# Introduction

Keith and I returned from another late night of cleaning a rental. Although it was late and I was dog tired, I scurried upstairs and turned on my computer. I had to write down some of the thoughts that were running through my mind like scared rabbits. By morning, they would be long gone. I had something to say and I wanted to get it on paper. I don't why I get inspired by cleaning up a vacant house, but every time I clean I get glimpses of how to be a better landlord, how to make more money and how not to be the one to clean the toilets when the next renter vacates the property. Most importantly, I want to share that knowledge with others so they will seize opportunities in real estate and in so doing benefit everyone concerned – the landlord, the renter and the community.

This book is to encourage those who are new to the rental business - to be great landlords, make money, invest locally, and treat tenants fairly. It"s possible to do all of these at the same time.

If people who are morally responsible own rental properties, most likely they will take care of them. They will not allow their properties to become run down. They will make timely repairs. They will provide decent housing for the poor. Gangs will not be attracted to areas of our cities because of broken windows, trash in the yards and caved in front porches. Children will be safe in their homes and in the streets. Having morally responsible people enter the rental market is good for America.

If only non-caring people who are out for the short-term bottom line are landlords, then this country will continue to have issues with neighborhoods spiraling downhill and rising crime rates. I personally would like to stop that from happening by helping caring, conscientious people of integrity own rental properties. This book is a small beginning for such a huge task, but it is just that, a beginning. We have to start somewhere. Why not start with you and me?

In this day when the moral fiber of our country is waning, there needs to come forth a group of individuals who are morally responsible and who will take being a landlord as a calling as well as a business. These are landlords who will take the challenge to be different from the stereotypical slumlord. Absentee landlords have created a crisis in America. People who own apartment complexes and houses often live across the country or even in another nation far away from their holdings. They hire big property management firms to interface with the tenants. While this is not bad in whole, there often is a gap where the "hands-on" landlord is needed. We want people who care about others to fill that gap.

I believe God wants us to prosper and to make money in all our investments, but He doesn't want us to make money at the expense of others. The good news is it's possible to make money and be fair to others. That is what we want to help you see by looking at a different way to manage your rentals. We encourage you to be a great investor, one whom God can bless. And we challenge you. Don't wait for change in this country - be the change!

# Needed - Local Landlords

On the evening of January 7, 2013, four women were found murdered in Fairmont Terrace, an apartment complex in Tulsa, Oklahoma. The bodies were not discovered until noon the next day when someone who lived near-by went to the apartment to check on the women. The only person alive in the residence was the three-year-old son of one of the victims who had most likely witnessed the killings. What had happened? The women were well liked and there was no apparent motive. Since multiple homicides are rare in Tulsa, the whole community was in shock.

Tulsa's major newspaper, *Tulsa World* carried headlines of the murders and the progress of the police investigation for six consecutive days. Once suspects were identified, the headlines changed and the focus was on the apartments where the women were tenants and on the apartment owners. As it turned out, the apartments were owned by a holding company located in California. Prior to the California corporation's acquisition, Fairmont Terrace was owned by a company who had on its management staff a community liaison to help identify the needs of the tenants and handle their complaints. Lanny Endicott's non-profit organization, South Tulsa Neighborhood Connection, worked with that liaison to improve the living conditions of the people at Fairmont Terrace. He had made great progress. When the management changed to the owners of two California limited liability corporations, the liaison was dismissed and the programs that had been set up for the tenants were abandoned.

Lanny told a reporter, "One of my biggest frustrations is you can talk to the management and they're good people, they work hard – but they get intimidated and beat up a lot. And the piece that is missing is the owners." (*Tulsa World* January 8, 2013.)

The owners of Fairmont Terrace were cited for lack of maintenance on the facility, poor security, inadequate lighting, understaffed management and general inadequate upkeep. As the heat turned up on the California owners, they quickly arranged for the sale of the 336 unit apartment property to Midwest Development Partners LLC located in Joplin, Missouri. The Missouri LLC agreed to the deal partially based on the tax credits offered to them by the Oklahoma Housing Finance Agency.

Lanny is absolutely correct. It is the owners that hold the missing piece to the property. They are the ones who should be the first to demonstrate pride of ownership which translates to the tenants. In retrospect there were a lot of things the owners could have done to create a more secure environment for the people.

Six months after the murders, violent crime was down 30 percent from 2012, in the Fairmont Terrace neighborhood because of the cooperation of the management and the people, not because of increased police coverage. Tulsa Police Chief Chuck Jordan made a statement to the *Tulsa World* newspaper. He said, "…We've had varying degrees of cooperation from the management, depending on who that was. It's hard for the police department to effect social changes." (*Tulsa World* June 30, 2013.)

There is a strong case for the local ownership of rental property. Maybe it's a bit like the case for farmer's markets and locally grown produce, there's just a lot more love and concern for quality put into the end product. There is a great need for local landlords which provides an excellent opportunity for the beginning and small investor.

Oz Guinness, founder of Trinity Forum, an organization dedicated to influencing and changing culture, believes strongly that the bloody French Revolution in the 1700s was prompted by France's absentee landlords. Because the landlords were not around, the properties were ill maintained while the owners demanded large rents from people who were least able to pay. Could absentee landlordism be one of the contributing factors to the downward spiral in American culture? (Guinness believes that one of the major challenges of globalization is a loss of responsibility. Responsibility is linked to accountability through visibility meaning that as they become detached or absentee landlords and their only thought is geared to the investor and not the people affected by their decisions.)

Real estate in the United States is relatively inexpensive compared to many other countries of the world. Some nations even deny the right of their citizens to own private property. For these reasons, foreign investors gobble up our real estate. Along with these outside investors, America has its own set of investors who search the country for high yield, low cost real estate in less cosmopolitan areas like Oklahoma, Texas and Arkansas. Many large apartment complexes are not locally owned. The bulk of this has happened in the US over the past 30 years.

Absentee owners often have little or no personal contact with their tenants. They treat their holdings strictly as a moneymaking business, considering only the immediate bottom-line. Often there is little thought to long term property maintenance or to providing benefits for the tenants who occupy their holdings. There is a great need for landlords who care about their properties and the folks who rent them. Like it or not, owning rentals is a people business as well as a real estate business. Investors who care about their property, their tenants and making money can do all three. Rentals properly maintained can provide supplemental income well into a owner's retirement years.

While many people are aware that America needs a cultural revolution. Few have answers as to how to start and sustain one. I strongly believe that the way to start a cultural change is by encouraging small investors to own and manage their own properties. This alone would transform the way real estate is managed in this country. It could be one of the missing links to creating better communities for us and our children.

# You Can Be a Great Landlord – and Make Money Too

"Would you rent this house to me?"

I looked down from the top of the ladder to see a neatly dressed African-American couple in their mid-forties. They had come to look at a vacant rental Keith and I owned. I had let them In the front door, told them to look around and then climbed back on top of the ladder to finish my business of cleaning the dining-room chandelier. The next thing I knew they were standing at the foot of the ladder looking up at me.

"Of course, we will," I said. And quickly added, "if your credit is good."

The man cleared his throat and spoke a little louder. "Our credit is good. It's just that we have five children. Will that make a difference in your answer?"

"Well, this is a four bedroom house. The kids will have to double up on a bedroom or two. If they don't mind sharing, then that shouldn't be a problem." I taught school in the daytime so I had to make the most of my time while at the rental. I pointed toward the kitchen and said, "There's a rental application on the counter. Pick up one, fill it out, and we will check your credit. If it's good, then you can move in. When do you need the house?"

"The beginning of next month," the man said.

"Perfect. We would love to have you here."

That was the first time I met Larry and Suzie Golden. They rented our home and lived there for five years. They took excellent care of the property and left it clean when they moved. After the Goldens vacated the property, I didn't hear from them again until almost ten years. I ran into Larry in the tire department at a huge Wal-Mart in town. When Larry approached me, we were eye level but I didn't recognize him. I must have looked dazed.

"You don't remember me?" he said. "I'm Larry Golden. My wife, Suzie and I rented your house on Imperial. I have something I have wanted to tell you for ten years." He shuffled a bit and continued, "When Suzie and I came into your house and asked if you would rent to us, we had already been to seven houses that day. The landlords had all turned us down. We had suspected it was because we were African-American and added to that was the fact that we had five children. But you didn't miss a beat. You said right up front that you would let us have the house. I can't tell you how grateful we were to you and your husband for renting to us. We were desperate to find a nice home and you allowed us to live in your house and you never acted like the color of our skin, or the number of kids we had bothered you."

I was a bit stunned but thanked Larry for the compliment and went about my business. I've found that landlords and teachers (of which, Keith and I are both: he taught college level math and I was a high school math teacher) get few "thank yous" so we relish each one we receive.

Keith and I have been privileged to be in real estate and the rental business for almost 40 years. We have met many nice people like the Goldens and we have also kissed many frogs along the way. Through it all, we have learned a lot. Now, for the nitty-gritty of a few of the lessons we have acquired along the way.

**The Positive Side of Rentals**

Since we have some knowledge in owning rentals, frequently people ask Keith and me questions about the real estate business. Keith is a Licensed Broker in Oklahoma and he doesn't mind answering any questions he can. People most often want to know how we got involved with buying homes, what we think about them, and how much trouble they have caused us.

Those who inquire often mention that they have at least considered rentals as a way to create cash flow or passive income but promptly dismissed the idea. Their knowledge of rental properties was based on negative reports they had heard from disgruntled landlords, who were happy to tell anyone who would listen about the bad tenant they had or how dirty the toilet was in the last house their tenant had vacated. Many times those who are telling the negative side of owning rental property fail to tell about the positive cash flow they received as a landlord, the tax breaks, capital gains and the many good tenants they have had through the years.

Life is what you make it and although you may run across disgruntled landlords and tenants who are not the best, you will encounter other tenants who are nice folks who need to rent from you. We've proven that you can be a good landlord and increase financially too. A lot of people are very rich today because they invested in rentals as a way to increase their wealth. In business, as in life, it is important to view the opportunities you have been given in a positive light and not curse the very thing that could make you happy and provide a nice income for you and your family, while enabling you to help others.

Owning rentals is a people business. You deal with people every time you lease a property. In many professions, dealing with people is a major factor that requires quite a few more people skills than being a landlord. Try being a doctor, a sales clerk, or a waiter/waitress. Be grateful and see your tenants in the light of what they are providing for you and refuse to listen to those who have nothing but negative things to say about owning rentals.

Because our almost 40 years of experience with our rental homes over all has been good, we know there is a positive side and encourage you to consider rental homes as a viable business that will, if done correctly, provide you with a good income. As a matter of fact, I created this book for people just like you - the small investor who wants to begin but doesn't know what to do or what to expect on the journey. I will give you the basic knowledge necessary to start so you can have a profitable rental business and your landlord experience will be a positive one.

## A Win-Win Situation

Keith and I began our real estate career in Denver, Colorado in 1975, fixing up properties and flipping them for profit. Our first house was built in 1898 and no one wanted to purchase it because it was believed to be haunted. We bought that "haunted" house and made money on it. Then in 1993, we bought our first rental, which we still have today.

We also own a real estate company, Global Network Realty, located in Tulsa, Oklahoma. Our company specializes in helping small investors who want to purchase residential homes as rentals. We've included our contact information at the end of the book. You may contact us at any time to find out more about how to get started on your journey to owning rentals and helping people while creating passive income for you and your family.

We meet people from every walk of life that we never would have had the opportunity to meet had we not rented a home to them. We have been able to provide a service and receive compensation for that service. Isn't that what a business is all about? It's a win-win situation. Let us help you to win.

When we started, we had no one to teach us, so we did a lot of things the hard way and we made mistakes along the way. Starting out, we both had full time jobs- I taught high school mathematics and Keith worked as a supervisor in the IT department of an oil company. When a property would become vacant, we would literally fall off the face of the earth, not to be seen by friends, family, or enemies for weeks on end while we cleaned, painted, mowed, wallpapered, and whatever else needed to be done until we had the property ready to rent again. We were not dummies and realized that with rentals, time is money. Since we didn't have a lot of money, we tried as best we could to leverage our time.

When you start out, you may be in the same boat as we were - we couldn't afford to hire all the work we needed done and it had to be done right and done quickly, so we did it ourselves. We didn't have time to search for the repair person who would do the job properly the first time (this will be one of the challenges you will face in the beginning but will become easier as you transition from the do-it-yourself mind-set to the I-will-not-clean-the-toilet mindset).

We also had the mind-set that we had purchased a home to rent when we should have thought of it as the first step in starting a business. It would have helped us to make more businesslike decisions as we went forward with the purchase of more rentals.

Because we have learned so much in our careers, we have compassion for those who are starting out with rentals as an investment. There is not much good advice in the marketplace for those who want to become successful landlords. You will find that there's a lot written for those who want to own property. Our objective is to help you be successful as a landlord *and* as a property owner. So learn from our mistakes, because we think we have made them all!

## Transition Rentals to a Business

Toilet cleaning is actually what inspired the idea for this book. Every time I would bend over a stinking toilet to clean it, I would think of all the ways I could have avoided that nasty task. It's not a pleasant position. I would tell myself, *"I know how to not be here, so why am I still here doing this?"* I realized that even with nine rentals, we still considered ourselves as individuals who had purchased nine homes to rent rather than our being in the business of owing rentals and being successful landlords. Finally I decided, *"I will transition our rentals to a business. I can do it!"* It wasn't easy but with determination I learned the basics. I did find that knowledge in and of itself is not enough. There has to be action to the transition and although the know-how is simple, the actual process of creating a rental business requires work.

A lot of landlords quickly abandon rentals after a nasty clean-up and for some their first one is their last. A friend of ours purchased a rental and after the first tenant left he said, "I will never clean up someone else's urine again!" That was the end of his rental career.

Others have told us, "I don't want to get a phone call in the middle of the night to go repair someone's clogged up toilet. So that's why I don't want to own rentals." Unfortunately, their perception of tenants and rental properties in general, have blocked out a great source of passive income that could be made available to them. Often we hear people like these friends complain about the less than 1 percent interest they are getting on their CDs.

We can honestly say that we have never received a call in the middle of the night to come to a property to unplug a toilet. Overall, we have found rental properties to be a great investment. As with any investment, you have to tend to it. We would certainly be misleading you if we told you that you could own property without any work on your part. The secret is that you learn to manage your rental investments in such a way as to make your experience as pleasant as possible while giving you cash flow. As with any investment, you are the best manager because no one better than you has your best interest at heart when it comes to your money.

### Rental Property vs. Stock Market - Our Story

I will never forget the day Keith and I sat across the desk from our financial advisor - *you know, the one who says he will manage your retirement money like his own.* We listened as he told us that we had just lost $350,000 over the last six months because of a downturn in the stock market. We were shocked at his nonchalant attitude. After informing us of the loss, which to us was an enormous hit, his next question was, "How do you want me to invest the remainder of your account?"

Now, I don't know about you, but we were not real anxious to take his word for his next series of investments suggestions. We were already considering real estate as a viable alternative because over our married life we had purchased several fixer-uppers and turned each one for a profit. Since we had never lost money in real estate, we left the advisor's office with a new resolve; (1) we were responsible for our financial future; (2) our future was in real estate.

If we had taken that $350,000 and purchased seven $50,000 homes (which were plentiful in our area during that time) our return on investment would have allowed us to make that money back in cash over the next 10 years; plus we would still own the properties along with an annual increase in equity and cash flow.

So if you are looking for passive and/or residual income, we believe that real estate, not the stock market, is the way to go. As a beginner, you may be a bit reticent about going forward. Work the numbers for what you need to retire and seriously consider rental investments as a viable option. We are not financial advisors, we are simply passing along our experiences and hoping that those experiences will help you make wise decisions about your future investments.

## Why We Believe Real Estate Is a Good Investment

Recently we had breakfast with a friend who had purchased a property in Oklahoma on a short sale. He paid $75,000 cash for a property that had appraised for $97,000. He can lease the property for $1200/month. When figuring the Return on Investment (ROI), he should come out very well. Let's look at his numbers.

$75,000   his investment

$22,000   his instant equity

($97,000 - $75,000)

At $1200/month his yearly income from rents will be $14,400, which will be reduced by the following expenses:

$1500   yearly taxes (estimated)
$1600   yearly insurance (estimated)
$1400   10% vacancy rate (estimated)
$4500   Total Expenses

Now let's see what his Return on Investment will be:

$14,000  Annual rents
$ 4,500  Annual expenses
$ 9,500  Annual Income

His estimated return on investment will be:

$9,500/$75,000 = 12.7%

In addition to his annual income, he will be able to deduct interest, taxes, and deprecation associated with this home on his income tax.

Plus he still has the $75,000 property and $22,000 in instant equity.

This is much better than if he put the money in a CD with interest at 2%, which would yield $1,500 for the year.

The property our friend purchased is in Tulsa, Oklahoma. While there are other areas of the country where purchasing rental properties is a good investment, we believe that Tulsa is one of the best. Housing prices in the Tulsa area have remained stable over the past ten years[1], making this an excellent area for the beginning investor. As such, you can find homes in a great price range that will give good ROI.

We also have found that the rental market in Tulsa is strong, which helps the beginning investor to be able to get a home rented in a short amount of time. Tulsa is a great place to start your rental business.

In his book, *Unfair Advantage: The Power of Financial Education,* Robert Kiyosaki, an investor, businessperson, and financial expert, included a section about his investment in an apartment complex in Broken Arrow, Oklahoma (which is located in Tulsa County). Part of his criteria for selecting that particular property was that it was located in a strong oil-based economy where jobs were plentiful.

**Start Your Journey**

Recently a lady applied to rent one of our homes who wanted to move out of a low rent housing complex into one of our rentals. Her main reason for wanting to rent from us was that we were small-time landlords and we were local. She had experienced the absentee landlord, who had little concern for his property and the people who rented from him. She was begging for a change.

---

[1] Kiyosaki, Robert T., The Unfair Advantage : The Power of Financial Education, Plata Publishing, LLC, Scottsdale, AZ, 2011, pg. 80.

We have followed ten simple rules in our business, that will help anyone become a good, profitable landlord without cleaning toilets. If you have to do it to start out in your real estate career, then purpose to stop when you get enough cash flow to pay to have someone else clean who does that for a living. Believe us, there is a way not to do it and we're going to tell you how. Just stick with us and hopefully we can make an unpleasant topic one that will be educational (as former teachers we are all into education!) and profitable for you and your new business of owning rental properties!

# Rule # 1: You Have a Business, Not a Hobby

If you have any interest in rentals, you have been subjected to an onslaught of invitations to seminars, put on by experts who want to tell you how to make quick and easy money in real estate. We have had our share of opportunities to pay huge amounts of money for someone to share his or her expertise with us on how to own rentals. One seminar stands out in our minds that made a profound effect on our real estate career.

It was while we lived in Denver in the late 1970s that we first attended a "Grow Rich in Real Estate" seminar. Frankly, neither of us remember the speaker's name, but he gave an illustration that still sticks with me today. He was very proud of the fact that he saved over $100 a year on his apartment complex expenses by getting rid of half of the garbage cans his renters used for disposing their trash. Since the amount of trash remained constant from the renters, the man went behind his apartments every night, took his foot and compacted the trash into the cans that were overflowing into the alley. It didn't matter that the renters had to wade through trash to get to the few garbage cans left.

The whole seminar was an exercise in how to squeeze more money out of the renters by providing fewer basic services and thereby putting more money in the landlord's pocket. We did not walk away with a good feeling about renters, landlords or owning real estate in general. That was just the opposite of what the speaker wanted from his audience.

In retrospect, the seminar speaker was appealing to the greed factor. Keith and I have never been susceptible to that vice. I believe that a lot of good landlords also have been turned off by the greed that has been perpetrated by those who think that everyone is like them—out to take the people who rent from them for everything they can. We believe that real estate profits can be made in fair treatment of tenants and thereby creating long term renters. That's why it is necessary to see your rentals as a business and not just as being an owner of multiple homes.

When you are just starting out in a rental business, it is very difficult to see yourself as a business owner. As I said earlier, in the beginning, Keith and I viewed ourselves as owners of multiple properties instead of owning a rental business. It took years for us to see our rentals as a legitimate business. We purchased all our rentals through government foreclosures. Most of the houses needed a lot of work, so we worked hard to clean, paint and make necessary repairs to be able to rent them quickly. At the time, we were both working full-time jobs—I was a teacher and Keith as a computer specialists trainer. We often worked all night long, went home and got ready for the next day's work. We wish someone had given us the advice in those early days that we are giving you now. Our toilet cleaning count would have been way, way down! It could have possibly saved our marriage a lot of wear and tear.

For the beginning landlord who has only a few houses, there has to be a switch turned on in your mind so you see yourself as a business owner rather than a rental homeowner.

*Remember, property management can be a royal headache if you let it.* Set some guidelines and whatever you do, start out right and stick by your plan of action. Set boundaries that will be workable for both you and your tenant. Most states have a free booklet on guidelines for landlords and tenants. It is detailed and cannot be consumed all in one setting. We suggest that you take it to the bathroom and read it in your spare time.

If you have a business, that means you, as an owner will:
- get paid by the first of the month
- not work on weekends
- do no plumbing or cleaning toilets on the weekends
- avoid the court systems because you will be wise and astute in choosing your tenants
- have few vacancies, minor maintenance and turnover because you manage your property and your tenants as a professional landlord
- arrange for routine maintenance, if you do, you will not be "surprised" by repairs and damage
- have a workable agreement between you and your tenant, thereby avoiding any and all personality conflicts that could potentially occur
- address each problem in a timely manner
- protect yourself legally

- update your contracts as they come due
- manage people instead of properties

**Remember that it is possible to lose money in any business.**

Regardless of what business you choose—pizza parlor, car repair, clowning for birthday parties, or anything else—if you do not run it right, it will fail. A business takes off and grows because someone is behind the steering wheel guiding it in the right direction. You must begin to see yourself in the correct light of a business owner in order to acquire more properties and increase your cash flow and net worth.

**Property Management 101**

Here are more guidelines to the rentals business that we recommend you put into practice.

**Buy only properties that you feel will rent easily and will appreciate in value.**

Buy, at a minimum, only two-bedroom, two-bath, two car garage homes in good neighborhoods. Yes, you can find those properties. Do not buy any property with structural damage.

**Manage people, not properties.**

Tenants are people. Without people, you have no business. Keep in mind that you are in the business of leasing to people. If you manage your tenants, and not just your properties, you will avoid many problems, particularly being taken to court or taking a tenant to court. Bear in mind that if you end up in court, you have failed as a people manager.

As human beings, tenants have ups and downs and everything in between. You will find some tenants who lie, cheat, and steal, but we can assure you, if you manage your tenants properly you will lessen substantially your having to deal with unscrupulous people. As many tenants will tell you, you can also find landlords who will lie, cheat, and steal. Those who are unscrupulous are on both sides of the rental spectrum.

We often scratch our heads at landlords who have nothing good to say about any of their tenants. They are always complaining about how the tenants are trying to do them in and how no one wants to pay rent. Frequently, that landlord is a person who is trying to squeeze every dime out of his or her property without investing time to screen tenants, develop relationships or manage people in an ethical manner. It is wise to always follow the Golden Rule when dealing with others—that is, treat others as you would want to be treated.

**Make sure you keep good records.**

You cannot run a business without keeping good records. Keep receipts of everything you purchase and every repair you have done to your house. Keep it in a file or on a computer if you are running a paperless office. The important thing is that you keep the receipts where you can find them easily.

Also keep a log of the times and miles you travel that pertain to your rental.

As for accounting software packages, we have tried several and found QuickBooks to be the best. One mistake we made when we first used QuickBooks was that we worked diligently on it for about a week, left it and didn't pick it up again for six months. We had to start all over again because everything we had initially learned was cold. Stay with whatever software package you use on a regular basis and you will learn how to use it faster. Blessed are you, if you already know how to navigate some kind of accounting software for rentals. You are far ahead of the pack.

**Never fall in love with your properties.**

If you are inclined to feel warm and fuzzy about a house that you have acquired and you just can't part with it, then go home and hold your dog. You must be objective about your properties. Be willing to sell a property when the right opportunity presents itself. Jesus told a parable about a Noble who gave three of his servants various amounts of money then went on a journey. When he returned as a King, he called the servants to find out what they each had done with the money in which they had been entrusted. The servant with the least amount of money had done nothing and was severely reprimanded. The other two servants had made money and were commended. Jesus makes a shocking statement when he demands the servant who had made no profit with his money turn over his small amount to the other two who had each made a profit (Luke 19:11–26). This is where Jesus makes the much controversial statement, "I tell you that to everyone who has, more will be given, but as for the one who has nothing, even what he has will be taken away." If Jesus said we should buy and sell and make a profit, then I also believe we should buy and sell houses for profit.

**Run a profit and loss statement every month.**

Part of the "buy and hold" mentality is that you never look at how your rental house is producing for you in terms of cash flow, appreciation on the property, loan amortization (the system for repaying the loan), and tax shelter benefits. If you never check, you could be holding on to something that is costing you money and you would not realize it. You will be like the frog who failed to jump out of the pot of boiling water—it got too comfortable when the water was warm and then when he wanted to jump, the water had already started to cook him. Jump at the right time and you will be more likely to win every time. However, you will never know when to jump unless you work out the numbers and find out if your property is costing you or bringing you money.

It would be a good practice to learn to run a profit and loss statement on your property or properties every month. You can find guidelines for profit and loss statements online, in your accounting software, or you can obtain a form from your accountant. You may even go to the bookstore or library and get a good book on investment property cash flow and read it through once or twice—and don't just read it but actually collect the data from your own property or prospective property and figure it out.

You cannot fly by the seat of your pants with rentals. As in any business, you have to work the numbers.

**Perform the necessary legal paperwork even before you need to do so.**

If it looks like you will have to evict someone, begin to prepare the legal notices and any necessary documentation before they are needed.

We have never had to evict a tenant. On occasion, we have had to ask people to move. When this happened, we tried to be diplomatic with the requests and so far that diplomacy has worked. We figure that it is to our detriment if we make a renter mad. That is a situation you want to avoid if at all possible. Once we had a renter leave owing us money, we took them to small claims court, and they paid what they owed. Don't threaten a tenant with small claims, just do it after they move. So having them move out on good terms and then going to small claims is our primary advice.

Our son, Jon, is a deputy sheriff. Frequently he tells us stories that the Sheriff's Department encounters in doing forced evictions. Recently, a deputy went to a property where the tenant was evicted and found holes knocked in the walls, appliances bashed in, paint spilled on the carpet, and all the lighting fixtures pulled out of the ceilings. We also have seen this with foreclosures. It's not a pretty sight when tenants leave angry. That's a situation you want to avoid at all cost. Often anger can be averted if you, the landlord, keep a cool head and deal with people diplomatically.

## Inspect your properties once a month—no matter what.

In our opinion (and that's why you are reading this book—for our opinions) there are only two reasons why you will want to evict a tenant faster than the speed of a bullet. The first reason is obvious and usually the one biggie that will get someone kicked out: they do not pay the rent. The second reason is not usually why renters are expelled, but I contend that it weighs in as heavily as failure to pay rent: they are abusing the property. Let us make it clear—they are not just abusing *a* property, they are abusing *your* property.

People who do not take care of property can literally break you. If you go on your property when it becomes vacant and find major abuse—like doors torn off the hinges, walls busted in, carpet with dog urine so thick that it squishes when you step on it, countertops beat up, and broken windows—all these things can cost you a lot of money, often much more than you ever took in for rent. As a caretaker of your property, you must look after it like your retirement depended on it, which it might if you are investing for cash flow retirement money.

Property abuse is one of the reasons why potential landlords shy away from investing in rentals. But in reality whose fault is it that the property was destroyed? My guess is that the landlord wanted to rent the property, shake the dust off his feet, collect the rent at the first of every month, and never look back. He bought into the lie that perpetrates the image of a big fat landlord who takes the rent and never makes an effort to inspect his property or make his renters accountable. Owning property requires active participation on the part of the owner; otherwise, you are asking for trouble.

Personal inspections are difficult because of time constraints. Keith and I are busy. When the first of the month rolls around and we have to make the trip to visit all of our properties, it becomes a real chore. Let's face it, we all like to take in the rent money but tending to the rest of the business can be a challenge.

It doesn't matter what you feel like. It's your property and you need to take the responsibility of checking on the houses that are in your name, you own, and more than likely you have the mortgage on—and that means you have financial liability if the property is not maintained.

**Make a checklist of things to look for on property inspections**.

Below is a short list of things you should be looking for when you do a monthly once-over of your property. This is the shortest list that you can possibly use and get by with calling yourself a landlord. It is the absolute minimum. Anything else and we will punish you by making you reread the chapter on becoming a socially responsible landlord!

_____ Furnace filter
(Has it been changed or do you need to change it?)
_____ Animal damage
_____ Number of animals at property
(Does it agree with the number on the lease agreement?)

_____ Number of occupants in the house
(Does it agree with the number of residents on the lease agreement?)
_____ Debris or trash around the house
_____ General overall care of property

**Accept Responsibility.**

Let me say a word here about responsibility. When you as a responsible person purchased the house you now rent, you assumed a certain amount of risk and along with that risk came responsibility. When my son, who is now 6 feet 2 inches tall, was two years old, and I was trying to teach him that his negative actions would result in bad consequences, I would say, "Jon, you are responsible for your own actions. If you stick your finger in the electrical outlet, you will get shocked. It is your responsibility to not do things that will cause you to get hurt."

He would often reply the only way a two-year-old can, "I don't want re-spons-i-bility." I marvel, because even at his early age, he knew that responsibility would require some self-discipline. Now as a grown man, he is a very responsible person. Thank God. But some of us never learn the valuable lesson that risk requires that we be responsible. Often things that happen are NOT someone else's fault—they are our own. If your properties are not taken care of, look at yourself in the mirror and say, "Now, how did I let that happen?" Nine times out of ten it will be your fault and not totally the fault of the renter.

It's okay to make mistakes (remember, we have made

them all), but when you do, you must be prepared to accept responsibility for your actions. If you allow individuals into your property without first checking with the last landlord they rented from, and they destroy your property, it will be your responsibility. Learn from your mistakes. Don't repeat them and don't blame someone else for what you did wrong. If you place your hand on a hot stove, you can't blame the stove. You will make some mistakes in your rental business, but you are on a journey and if you are willing to accept full responsibility for your errors, you will be successful.

# Rule # 2: Separate Business and Personal Expense

I love the jokes that I hear about lawyers, especially when they make a joke about themselves. Recently I was at a writer's conference and heard a lawyer speak about a new book he had written on the brain. He kept trying to convince the audience that he was telling the truth. Repeatedly he stated, "You have to trust me. This book I just wrote about not losing your memory is really good. I know I am a lawyer, but this time I'm telling the truth." Everyone laughed. Yet while lawyers may have a bad reputation for not telling the truth, the truth is that you will need some good legal advice when you begin your rental business.

You will need to seek out a lawyer and do what he or she says, but Keith and I are telling you some things that would have saved us a lot of heartache. Ask your lawyer about putting your rentals in a Trust or Limited Liability Company (LLC) and move them as quickly as possible away from your own personal credit. I may sound like a broken record, but we can't emphasize this enough: make your rentals a business—treat them as a business and financially act as though they were a business.

You may not be able to do this at the onset of your career as a rental property owner, but you can have it in mind and move in that direction as you progress. We have talked to the accountants of rental property investors who had many clients who never put their properties into a legal entity. Besides the personal liability, if a renter is clumsy and should conk his head on your door frame and sues you because you made his IQ go down ten points, the debt liability you would have should scare you enough to make you listen to us.

It only takes a minimum amount of money to do a name search for your new real estate rental company and to set up a LLC in that name. Of course, once you have it set up you will have to fund it. You do this by opening a checking account in your new company's name, then putting some money in that new company, and paying for related expenses out of that account. Doing those things may even help you see yourself as owning a new business. Now you are a true real estate investor!

Once you have some money in your new business account, take out a credit card at a home improvement store in that new company name. Imagine that all your properties will be turned back over to you with no need of repairs so you will never have to use that precious credit card. However, the reality is that you will need to do some maintenance and when you do; you will have your new credit card available. You are establishing credit in the name of your business. Eventually you will move all of your business related credit to your company and it will not reflect on your personal credit.

**You Can Succeed!**

We recommend that you put money into your business account on a monthly basis. This is money you will use to purchase more rentals and you will be amazed at how fast the money grows as you stash a little away each month. It won't be an overnight success, but it will be a success. Trust us on this. We are not lawyers and our lie index is very low!

Because we didn't set up a trust in which we could purchase our rentals, we bought all of our first homes with mortgages as a result all expenses incurred with those purchases were treated as personal expenses. It is best if you purchase in a trust or LLC from the beginning, but sometimes that is not possible. Everyone in the rental business should discuss the purchase of any property with a proper attorney and tax professional.

We cannot advise you legally in this area. Our concern is that you treat your rentals as a business. Start out with that mind-set and you will eliminate a lot of problems and wrong misconceptions.

People either fail or succeed in business every day. There is a fine line that separates failing from succeeding and the way you set up your business and the records you keep, or don't keep, will help you succeed or fail. If you only have one rental, you have a business. Treat it as such. It will prove to be a great training ground as you grow your properties from one to two, then to the number you need to meet your financial goals.

# Rule # 3: Select Good Tenants

Keith and I met for dinner after he had shown one of our properties to a potential renter. He opened his file with the new application in it to show me and was excited when he told me how great the prospect was: "This lady is so good, I can't believe it!" His excitement made me feel like this rental would be leased quickly and that meant that we would rent in record time, have our money in the bank, and all our houses occupied with great, gainfully employed renters.

Anticipating the wonderful news that was following, I blurted out the most important question in my mind: "Does she have a job?"

"Well," he hesitated, "no, not exactly."

"What does that mean?" My anticipation quickly made a leap to aggravation.

Keith paused and tried very hard to choose the right words. "She doesn't have a job. She is recently divorced from a doctor who is able and willing to pay a lot of alimony and child support."

I was not one to be impressed with the simple fact that someone is a doctor and being in the medical profession means that person is also moral, upstanding, and pays all his or her bills. "Well, we'll have to run a credit report," I said.

On the defensive, Keith gave a quick response. "Hear me out. They have the money and she will pay. She is a nurse herself and plans on getting a job as quickly as possible. I hate to spend a half day running a credit report and have her pay the $35. Why don't we just rent it to her? She wants to move in this weekend." Keith watched to see my reaction and then ventured a little further. "She will pay the deposit, first month's rent, and on Monday when she gets the money from her ex-husband, she will pay the last month's rent. Without even my asking, she volunteered all that."

While it sounded so enticing, especially since this was Thursday and the house could be rented by the weekend, I still had a reality check. I remembered once before, not too long ago, a lady who wanted to rent from us. She was a family counselor and kept foster children to boot; she also had a great income and looked like a benevolent person who loved kids and wanted families to stick together. However, when a credit report was run on her, it was horrible. It looked like the lady had never paid for anything in her life. She had over forty uncollected checks for things like pizza, Avon, and manicures and that didn't include all the late payments, car repossessions, and credit card defaults noted on the report. When Keith called her to tell her that we wouldn't rent to her, I was shocked when I overheard him ask, "Lady, have you ever paid for anything?"

With that experience in mind, I said about the nurse, "I'll run the credit report tomorrow, that way she can still move in on Saturday if it looks okay."

The next day I trudged begrudgingly to the office to run the credit report. When the final report came, I could hardly wait until Keith got home to show him. Evidently this wasn't the first time for this lady to leave her husband, rent a house and try to start a new life. Her credit report was twenty pages long on not-so-good items. Needless to say, we didn't rent to her and we waited until someone came along who could pay the rent.

**Getting the First Tenant**

Getting the first tenant is always the scariest. No matter how much you prepare for the screening process, there is always a measure of uncertainty. When someone calls on your sign or ad, have a checklist in front of you so you won't leave anything out that you or the potential tenant will need to know. Here are a few items that you should relay when talking to a potential tenant:

- Street address of the property
- Monthly rental amount
- Deposit amount (if you are willing to split the deposit over two months, tell them)
- Number of bedrooms
- Number of bathrooms
- Garages
- Fencing

- Neighborhood schools

- Term of lease

- Pets—will you allow them or not and any restrictions you have on pets (Often insurance companies do not allow certain types of pets- exotic animals, Pit Bulls, Rottweiler's, etc. Because of this restriction we immediately tell potential tenants what our restrictions are. We allow one pet with no extra deposit and $250 for every pet after the first.)

- Do you take low income government assistance—as Section 8?

If you get a lot of calls without anyone wanting to look at the house, you might consider coming down on the amount of monthly rent you are requiring. We will come down in $50 increments until we get a viable tenant. Keep your ear tuned with what the market will bear. We have had people try to negotiate a lower rent with us and on occasions we have acquiesced and rented for the lesser amount. When we do this, it is with good reason. The renter was well qualified (and could prove it). Our thinking was that it was better to rent to them than to wait for a less qualified tenant. It's your call, and you will get better with it as you acquire more experience.

One way to make a decision on whether or not to take $50 a month less than what you are asking is to ask yourself, *If I wait another month without renting this house, how much money will it cost me?* If you are asking $1,000 a month rent, it will take you 20 months to make up for one month's vacancy.

Whether or not you decide to lower the monthly rent, ask the potential renter for three things:
1. Proof of income or employment verification

    This form should be filled out by the potential tenant's employer and faxed back to you. It should include the date, name of employee, employer, a request to the employer that says something like, "with this letter please release the following information to (your name), date of employment, current monthly salary, signature line for potential tenant, tenant's social security number.

2. Permission to run a credit report and background check

    Here is what we put on the form that the potential tenants sign: current date, full legal name, home phone number. cell number, social security number, current address and how long they have resided at that address, email address (required), repeat this information for spouse or any other adult occupant, number of children and ages, number of pets and type/breed, credit references which will include the current landlord and one other reference

    Along with this information, I add the following statement: "I hereby certify that all the statements made above are for the purpose of obtaining credit and are true and complete, and I authorize you to seek any of my creditors to give such information as you may require, and agree that this application shall remain your property. Credit reports will be obtained by (Your Name).

Signature lines for each applicant

3. Current residence verification

On this form I include the following to be filled out by the prospective tenant: current date, current landlord's name, address of property, name of tenant,

Ask the following information from the current landlord: term of residence: monthly rent; frequency of late payments, care of leased property, would you lease to this person again? current landlord's signature, This information should be faxed back to you in a timely manner. Be sure you have your potential tenant sign the form.

**Running Background Checks**

Remember our story at the beginning of this section? Let that be a lesson to you. Always, always run a credit report on a potential renter! In the past we have used an on-line company called SmartMove ([www.mysmartmove.com](www.mysmartmove.com)) for credit verifications. SmartMove is an arm of TransUnion Credit Reporting and will cost the potential tenant approximately $35 (at the time of this writing). It is a free service to a landlord, but you must sign up as a landlord in order to use it.

Currently we use a local businessman who does background screening. The cost is cheaper, results are back within 24 hours, and the report also gives information if the person has a criminal backgroundr. Any negative item may cause you to think twice about renting to someone.

**Should you look for a perfect credit report?**

Many people rent because they are having some type of credit problem and can't purchase a home at the moment. Occasionally you will find someone who is looking to rent because they are building a new home or they are getting a divorce and want to wait until the dust settles before purchasing a home. Many times people rent a property because they can't qualify for a mortgage. If they can get their credit straightened out, then they usually go on to homeownership. Therefore, we don't look for squeaky clean credit. But what we do look for is some inclination that they are trying to pay their bills. So you have to give them some leeway.

What you are really looking for when you view a credit report is that they have a good payment history. Often people who rent have gotten behind in their bills and you as a landlord must take a close look to discover the reason for their past late payments. What we see most often are unpaid medical bills. What you don't want to see on a credit report are red flags like bad checks for not paying the pizza delivery man. Have a bit of compassion and try not to be so black and white. Potential tenants are human beings—treat them as such. We all have made mistakes and most of us have had financial difficulties at one time or another.

When you have questions about items on a credit report, have a discussion with the potential tenant as to why their credit score wasn't so good. If there is a logical explanation, make a judgment after you have heard their story.

If you see a problem you can't fully satisfy with a one-on-one conversation, follow up your credit report with necessary phone calls, beginning with calling the last person from whom your potential renter leased. This is a simple thing to do and may end up being the best call you ever made.

# Rule # 4: Make Timely Repairs

When I was a kid, I loved the short mini-movies that ran before the "real" movie started. One of my favorite clips was of Ma and Pa Kettle. This series was old when I was young so you may not remember them. Ma and Pa had 11 children that were continually getting into trouble. Ma was the take-charge sensible one who took care of every emergency. Pa was the passive aggressive father who stood by and looked on while the kids burned down the barn. He would say in a monotone voice, "Ma, the kids are burning down the barn," while huge flames leapt from the barn roof. Ma was the one who would immediately organize the bucket brigade and get the fire under control.

With your rental properties you can be the take-charge person like Ma or you can be the passive aggressive type like Pa. If you are the latter, guesses are you will run into bigger and bigger problems because you put things off. Learn to tackle problems as they happen and not stand and look at the barn burning.

**Make a List**

The best way to avoid being like Pa is to make a list of the repairs that either you know need to be done or that your renter has told you needs to be done. If a renter calls and says there is a small tear in the fence, it may not warrant your making a trip all the way out to the property to check, at least not at the moment. Put it on your list and when you make your monthly property inspections, take care of the small tear in the fence. Taking care of small items will save you lots of money in the long run. If you don't put the smallest things on a list, most likely you will forget them and let them slide until the dog bursts through the fence and the whole panel has to be replaced.

A little diligence goes a long way. Minor maintenance can eat your lunch if you do not manage it quickly. So keeping a log of your properties and the calls your renters make to you with complaints of repairs that need to be made (big and small) is essential. Remember, don't let things linger and not take care of them. The small leak in the roof can turn into a huge leak that will require more money and effort to repair. This applies particularly to toilets. When a renter tells you a toilet is leaking, take care of it. If you don't, for sure you will have your head behind the stool trying to fix something that started out small and ended up being a huge mess that not even a decent plumber wants to tackle. Be diligent and proactive with necessary repairs. Don't put them off.

Here's the bottom line: If you don't want to end up replacing toilets and cleaning up huge messes, take care of the little repairs in a timely manner. Your ultimate goal is to avoid the Big Three—vacancy, major maintenance, and turnover.

**Change the Furnace Filter Regularly**

If you don't already know it, I will tell you now, renters seldom change furnace filters. No matter how often you explain to them all the money it will save them on electric bills or how much cleaner the air inside the house will be, they just don't do it. We have purchased enough filters for a rental for a year only to come back the next year and find 12 filters sitting neatly by the furnace. You guessed it—the same twelve filters. We also tell our renters that when those run out we will replenish them if they want to change their own filters.

You may be wondering how this fits into the repairs category. If you change your furnace filter once a month, you stand a good chance of preserving the life of your furnace and air conditioner. This will save you big bucks in the long run as those are two of the most expensive replacement items in your house that insurance will not cover if they break down. Once you realize the cost from not changing filters, you will run, not walk, to the nearest home improvement store, purchase some filters, and be at the front door of your rental on the first of every month.

So now that you know your tenant will likely not change the filter, that chore remains for you, the landlord, to perform or for someone you have hired. This should be easy to do because you are going to inspect your property once a month anyway and when you go on the premises you can also change the filter. Actually, changing the filter will give you a good excuse to go to the home and while you are there changing the filter, you can look at the way they are caring for the rest of the house. And don't forget to do an animal headcount while you are looking around!

***We recommend that you make a checklist of things you are looking for when you inspect the property each month***. See the list I gave you under Property Inspection to help you evaluate your property.

Your tenants will most likely take better care of your property if you do. If you have a reputation for not taking care of your properties, any chance you had of your renter doing so will go down the drain. Your ultimate success in the rental business will be determined by how well you manage your tenants. If all landlords were good managers, there would be no need for the federal and state governments to pass rules and laws that make landlords do things they should do as a matter of diligence.

# Rule # 5: Keep Rents and Repairs Separate

I once worked in a real estate office with Mark, a stereotypical landlord who appeared to be without a shred of compassion. Often Mark would allow a tenant to move in a home that desperately needed cleaning and painting with the agreement that the new renter would do some work on the property and in exchange Mark would take $100 off the first month's rent. Occasionally I witnessed firsthand the consequences of this, like the time I went to one of Mark's rentals and the inside walls of the home were painted with black enamel paint. Mark did not come out ahead on that agreement.

Keith and I have found these types of agreements to be unprofessional and unbeneficial to us as homeowners. There are two reasons for this.

First, *the renter may not know how to do the repairs.* This would make the situation worse. Think about it: you are agreeing to let someone paint, repair or otherwise fix something of yours that potentially is worth over $100,000. Not everyone knows how to paint a room and certainly what is clean for one person is not always clean to another.

I have looked at some paint jobs and wondered why the paint store associate sold that person the paint in the first place. When the tenant doesn't tape off the area to be painted so that paint doesn't get on the woodwork, you have paint splattered on the door facings, doors, and worse yet, the carpet. This alone could cause you problems since a blotched paint job can be difficult, if not impossible, to repair. If you want to sell the property later, you have to correct someone else's mistakes in order to make your property saleable. Have you ever tried to paint walls covered in black enamel paint? That's my point exactly.

Secondly, *accounting gets more complicated when you exchange work for rent.* My mother owned several rental properties. She was business savvy and no one messed with her, especially not her renters. She was blind in her later years, but didn't let that stop her. She knocked on the door of her rentals at the first of the month and they knew they had better have the rent money in hand. She never cleaned a toilet in any of her rental houses. We should have learned from her how not to clean toilets, but we learned the hard way.

One thing my mother never did was let a renter exchange work for rent. She would always say, "Rent is rent and work is work. You pay the rent and I pay for work." She never mixed the two. Even if a renter did some repairs on the property, she paid them immediately on the spot out of her rental account.

Now, you probably are going to say, "What if I rent to a painter? What then? Surely I can let a 'professional' paint." We're telling you, think twice and make sure they know what they are doing; just like you were hiring a painter, you would check references. Pay them for their work and do not deduct it from the rent.

This may seem to have little to do with getting your

head from behind the toilet, but it has a lot to do with maintaining your property. There are some jobs that need to be done by licensed professionals, like switching out electrical plugs—be sure you are covered legally by hiring an electrician. Still, you should make sure all repairs are done properly and that you do not have a bum repair job that someone has done and charged you for. You can check what has been done and give your approval or you can stay with a repairman to make sure he has done the job he came to your house to do.

Be proactive with maintaining your properties. Legally a renter has the right to repair some things that you may have been lazy about getting done and then subtracting that expense from the rent. So in order to avoid this, you need to get the repairs done quickly—and whenever possible, professionally.

# Rule # 6: Find Excellent, Dependable Contractors

I once called about an apartment building for sale and in the course of the conversation with the selling agent, found that the reason the owner was selling was because he was losing money hand over fist. It seems that this out-of-state owner had contracted with a managing company that was charging him $250 per light bulb change. Since the owner was 1,500 miles away, he was not able to visit the property and he wasn't familiar enough with the area to know whom he could trust or if the price he was charged was reasonable.

It is a lesson to all of us to look high and low to find repair people with good reputations who will repair items quickly and not overcharge for their services. This also applies to management firms when we come to the place in our businesses when we need their services.

My mom had a saying that is very appropriate when looking for a reliable, honest and fairly-priced repairperson: "They are as scarce as hen's teeth." Since hens have no teeth, you get my drift. They are hard to find and you have to be streetwise and business savvy to locate a trustworthy person who will do a good repair job. Once you find someone, treat him or her with respect. Pay your bills on time and talk nicely when you call them.

Here is a partial list of people you will need to have in your repairs bank:

Plummer

Electrician

Exterminator

Tree Removal Person

House Cleaner

Yard Maintenance Person

All-around Handyman

Air Conditioner/Furnace Repairperson

Locksmith

Painter

Hopefully, you will be able to combine some of the above categories and build a good reputation faster with fewer persons. To help you get started, here are some of our favorite places to find good repair people:

1. By far the best way to find someone is to ask a friend for a reference. We found excellent repair people by asking friends for recommendations.
2. Ask other landlords who they use to repair their furnace or air conditioners. Call several people and do it before the need arises. Make notes of

your friends' comments and listen when they say, "He did a great job on repairing the A/C but...." Weigh the "buts" you hear and decide if this person is a fit for what you are looking for. Just because you hired someone once, you don't have to hire that same person again to do another job for you. You are the boss.

3. Ask real estate agents who they use for repairs. A lady who owned a real estate brokerage firm and had firsthand knowledge of repair people who had done good jobs for her clients, supplied us with at least three of the people on our list. And those three have stayed with us for almost twenty years.
4. Whenever you see a completed job and you admire the workmanship, ask who did the work.
5. Check online sites for repairmen with good reviews.

*Calling someone out of the Yellow Pages is one of the riskiest things you can do.*

## Schedule Yearly Furnace and Air Conditioning Inspections

Remember my suggestions about changing out your furnace filters because if you do that you will save a lot of money in repairs? Equally as important as the monthly filter change is finding a reputable air conditioner company and scheduling yearly inspections of your furnaces and air conditioning units. Put it on your calendar. We schedule maintenance in the late spring when the A/C person isn't so busy and the temperatures are high enough to test air conditioning units.

# Rule # 7: Know When to Transition to a Property Management Company

When you have enough positive cash flow, you can afford to have someone manage your properties. If you started out small, like we did, then this may take some time. Once you come to that point, make sure you hire a reputable company that has good references. Even so, you should always inspect the property after a tenant has vacated the home, especially in the beginning.

Make a list of all the work you want the company you hire to do. That way both of you will know exactly what to expect. And it will help you negotiate the price for their services. If they charge every time they visit one of your houses, ask what that fee per house will be and have it in writing. The bill can often grow if you don't set a price before the work starts. We have already mentioned the management company that charges $250 to send someone out to a rental to change a light bulb. You don't want that. So make sure you know the charges before you sign a contract with a management company.

Some landlords never want to turn over their property management to someone else. We know a man in his nineties who takes care of his own properties. One thing in his favor is that over the years, he has found great cleaners, painters, and repairpersons. You may want to do the same. That's your call.

We've mentioned how some people say they don't want the hassle of rentals. They do not want to clean toilets and get calls in the middle of the night. We can't think of one business where you don't have hassles—and most business have toilets. Hassles are hassles although they are sometimes called by different names, so if you own or desire to own rental properties, just get used to the fact that you will have some hassles. The trick is learning how to handle the difficulties and having the right team around you to help in time of need.

We have included a checklist for your cleanup crew at the end of the book. This list will help you know the areas on which to focus.

## If You Don't Have Time to Inspect Your Properties, Hire Someone

If you don't want to use a management company and you hire your own contractors, don't forget to hire someone to inspect your properties on a regular basis. Make sure you trust their judgment. But if you are just starting out in the rental business and are on a shoestring budget, wait until you get enough cash flow to hire someone. Make sure the person who is doing the inspection knows what you are looking for and gives you a written report on what he or she finds so you can follow up when needed.

Keep in mind that if you hire someone to clean or inspect your properties, it is a business expense and is tax deductable. If you do it yourself, it is not.

## What to Expect of a Property Management Company

A property management company should provide you with the most income possible. Make sure you check with other landlords who are using property management companies and get good references before you sign a contract with anyone.

Here are some things you should expect a company to do:

1. Collect the monthly rent.
2. Direct deposit the monthly rents into your banking account.
3. Arrange for maintenance repairs (make sure you know who the company is using for repairs and that their prices are reasonable).
4. Give you good advice on what your house should bring in monthly rents. They should know what comparable properties in your area are charging.
5. Provide you with a professional lease and lease renewal forms.
6. Get your property ready for a new tenant.
7. File eviction notices if needed.
8. Obtain from potential tenants a credit report, employment and rental history.
9. Negotiate the lease.
10. Send late notices to a tenant who has not paid on time.
11. Receive and tend to all emergency calls.
12. Provide you with monthly accounting for your property.

13. Market and advertise the property.
14. Inspect your property, should you request the service.
15. Change the furnace filters monthly, should you request the service.

The going rate in the Tulsa area for property managers is 10% of the monthly rents and approximately 75% of one month's rent when a new tenant is placed in your rental (at the time of this writing). Some companies charge 100% of a month's rent for placing a new tenant. You will need to shop around for the best price.

It is important as a beginning landlord that you not totally turn your property over to a management company. You must remain actively involved or else you will be just like the person who turns all your retirement accounts over to a money manager and expects him or her to have your best interest at heart. Remember that the company is probably managing a lot of other properties as well as yours. You will need to check on your properties and stay abreast of what is transpiring with them.

# Rule # 8: Never Spend All Your Cash Flow

"We have twenty four hours to move," she told us, teary-eyed and near panic. She was about thirty years old, a single mother with two children. The Sheriff's Department had come by that day and spoken with her.

"Our house is being sold tomorrow at the Sheriff's Auction at the courthouse," she said, "and we just got notice today that we absolutely must move tomorrow. We paid the rent every month. We never expected this to happen. About six months ago we got a notice that the house was in foreclosure. I called the landlord who told me to continue to pay the rent because he was working things out with the mortgage company and everything would be okay. We never heard anything else from the mortgage company so I thought it all had been taken care of.

"I have to stay in this neighborhood because of the school my kids are in and with only one more month of school I can't move them out of this district. I don't know what to do."

We felt sorry for her. We had at least another week of work to do before our rental would be move-in ready. The lady left our house and when we contacted her later to let her know that our house was ready, she had already found a place to move. That was not the first time we had heard this story. We have had many potential tenants come to view a home we have for rent and tell us something similar. Most of the time they have at least seven days to vacate their property, but this lady only had one day. No wonder she was about to cry.

This problem has become more common since the 2008 housing crisis. The landlord could have avoided creating that catastrophe if he had purchased only properties with a positive cash flow when rented and if he had not spent that cash flow from his rents.

If we had to say which of our rules was the most important, this would be the one. We know from personal experience. So we're telling you what to do here to keep you from biting your nails every time a renter moves out until you see if you have enough money to cover the mortgages while you get the house up to speed and new renters located.

As you start out, you may not have the reserves you would like, but if you follow our advice (remember, we've been there and know a few of the ropes), you will not go wrong. If you begin without enough in reserve, realize that you are taking a huge risk and be prepared when you have to pay for repairs out of your own pocket or come up with a mortgage payment when the house is vacant. The point is that when the cash flow starts coming in, *do not* spend the cash flow.

Even if you only make $50 a month after you pay the taxes, mortgage, and insurance, put that money in a special account and save it until you have a reserve of at least $3,000 for each house you own. The $3,000 per property ($5,000 is better) should be your bare minimum for reserve. That will give you enough money to replace a furnace, air conditioner, or any other of your more expensive replacement items that insurance will not cover.

You might consider what it would take to maintain your property for six months, should it remain vacant for that long. We have never had a rental house stay vacant for six months, even in a slow market, but we have had one vacant for three. It can put a tremendous drain on your finances. Actually, one house unrented for six months may bankrupt a small rental business owner. So beware. Only after you have a decent reserve for your house can you even think about touching your cash flow.

This rule has everything to do with your not cleaning toilets because if you have a cash reserve for your house, then you will be able to hire a nice plumber to come and repair the toilets and a nice cleaning lady to come and clean them between vacancies. Just replace that money when it comes in from rents. Once your cash flow starts back up again you can replenish your reserve.

# Rule # 9 Craft a Great Lease Agreement

Do you know the joke about having an oral contract? It's worth the paper it is written on. Always remember that when you put together a lease, anything you can think of that you and your tenant agree on needs to be in writing. If you don't, most likely you will regret it at some juncture. It's just too risky to rely on memory when dealing with legal matters.

I suggest you go online to find an example of a lease that will be appropriate in your state. Our lease has evolved with us over the years as we've added clauses that pertain to items, like pets, where we have restrictions. It is always great to have legal advice anytime you put together a contract. Going to the local office supply store to purchase a packet of lease agreements is not what we recommend. You might try going online to find lease agreements, but ultimately, you will need to come up with a lease agreement that you are comfortable with using.

Here are some suggestions for creating a good lease agreement that you will like:

1. Use simple, clear, specific language.
2. Write everything on which you and the tenant agree in the lease.
3. Make at least two copies. Give a copy to the tenant and you keep the original.
4. Use 8 ½" by 11" paper. This makes your lease easier to file.
5. Ask the tenant to initial each page as an acknowledgement that he/she has read the content.

6. Adapt your lease to your situation.

Mark the date of the lease on your business calendar and two months prior to the expiration of the current lease, send the tenant a renewal lease. If you don't do this in Oklahoma, the lease reverts to a month-to-month lease. You will need to check what happens when a lease is expired in your state.

If you decide to inspect your property once a month, you will need to put that in the lease agreement as well. It will be good for your renter to know you might be there, even if you don't or can't come by for a month or two.

At the end of the book, I've included a checklist to go over while you are on the premises of your rental. You don't want to be too nitpicky but you want to make sure that you still have a house standing when your renters move. This checklist has helped me evaluate properties that Keith and I were going to flip. It serves as a great reference when I look at a property so that I don't overlook anything.

**Ter ms of Lease**

We do not rent for less than a year. There are a couple of reasons for that. It will take you as much time to get the property ready to rent again as it did for this renter. You could potentially have the property vacant twice in the same year and you don't want that.

We try to have the lease end in the late spring or early summer. These are prime renting times. Tenants generally do not look for a different home after their children are already enrolled in school and the parents are busy getting school clothes, supplies and school transportation established.

Something else we've found is that renters often have more difficulty coming up with a deposit than with the rent. So it is sometimes beneficial to allow a renter to pay a deposit over a two or three month period of time—whatever you are comfortable with doing. We feel that since moving is costly, often paying for the deposit in two or three monthly increments is very helpful. And we state how the deposit is dispersed in the lease agreement. This may sound risky, but we have never had anyone not pay us the deposit.

**Late Fees**

For years, we had our rents due on the twelfth of the month. Finally we got wiser and made them due on the first of the month and late on the fifth. Another thing that has helped us is that we make the late fee 10% of the monthly rent. So a house that rents for $800/month will have a late fee of $80. This has helped tremendously because when we started we would make the late fee $20, which wasn't enough of an incentive to encourage the tenant to pay on time. The $80 or 10% fee works much better for getting rents paid on time.

# Rule #10: Keep Count of Pets and Other Animals

Miss Calley was a retired school teacher who came across as a sweet little old lady. With her thick Cajun accent, she introduced us to her roommate: "This is Boulegard," she said as she petted the white toy poodle on the head. "He is the sweetest thing and stays right with me all the time. I call him my little roommate." Boulegard looked up at us with pleading eyes. We took to him right away and figured we were safe with him from any of the usual pet damage or excessive barking that would disturb the neighbors.

Little Boulegard turned out to be a lot stronger than those sad droopy eyes let on. When Miss Calley passed away a few months into her lease, and we went to prepare the house for the next tenant, we found that the little doggie seemed to have an affinity for carpet. He had dug up the carpet at the corners and chewed each one to a frazzled nub. We were horrified. Our lesson: you can never judge a pet by the size of its eyes.

As a landlord you will get numerous calls on your rental asking about whether or not you allow pets. So be prepared. Even if they don't ask you about pets, you need to bring up the question with them. This will save you a lot of time and trouble. It appears that most potential renters have at least one dog and a surprising number of them have two or more pets.

Recently I spoke with a lady who had four dogs and four cats and she was looking for a rental. Because the lady complained about the fact that landlords didn't want to rent to her, I suggested that she lessen the number of animals she owned. Her answer, "Well, my cats and doggies are just like family. I couldn't get rid of a one of them. Besides that, they are not like most animals; they are good and never create a mess." My thought was, *Really?* Needless to say, we didn't rent to this lady. Four dogs and four cats are way past our limit.

You will find out three things with rentals regarding pets:

1. Pets are like part of the family and renters will bring them to your property.
2. Renters will tell you that their dogs are outside dogs and never come in the house. That is usually not true.
3. Pets have a tendency to accumulate. When a renter leases a property, they may have one dog, but before you know it they get another dog and maybe a cat.

Animals are just that—animals. No matter how much they may act like a human, they are not. For the most part they are messy and do what animals do—make a house harder to keep clean. Keep that in mind when renting if you choose to allow pets.

## Pet Restrictions

We do not allow tenants to have the following dogs:

> Rottweiler
> Chow
> Pit Bull
> Great Dane
> Doberman
> Saint Bernard
> Labs
> German Shepherd

This restriction also applies to a dog with a dominant mix of any of these breeds.

While you may be coerced into wanting to rent to someone with one of these breeds, it is a decision you may not be able to make independently. Most likely your insurance company has a similar list and may not cover any incident where one of these breeds is involved. *Check your policy*. Our policy specifically bans the breeds on our list. Renters with these pets may not like your denying them the opportunity to rent, and you may not want to tell them no; but you can blame it on your insurance company, and you will be telling the truth. There's no middle ground here. When it comes to pets, you must be firm.

Something else we do not allow is reptiles (such as snakes, alligators, and lizards); nor do we allow birds. We made the bird decision after we had a friend whose rental was ruined because the tenant allowed the birds to have free reign in the house. The result was bird droppings everywhere and a smell that wouldn't go away.

Earlier I gave you the basics of our pet agreement for you to use as a guide. We allow one pet (exceptions listed above) with no extra deposit. After that we charge $250 for each additional pet.

When dealing with pets and rentals, you will need to count the animals when you make your monthly inspections. Unless you visit the property on a regular basis there is no other way you will know if the renters have more than the one pet they told you they had when they moved in. I am amazed at how renters who are struggling to pay their monthly rent can afford dogs. Not only that, but often the dogs are huge and frequently there are multiple dogs. It's not that we hate animals. We love animals and have nothing against them, but from our own experience (and as landlords know) animals can damage a home overnight—scratching woodwork, chewing on and/or urinating on the carpet. We have had innocent little poodles (remember Boulegard) that would scratch holes in new carpet and big dogs, well, don't even get me started! **We include our pet agreement in the body of our lease. If you wish you can have a separate agreement.**

# Be a Socially Responsible Landlord

On one routine rental turnaround, we couldn't believe the horrible condition of the house. It was every landlord's nightmare. When I opened the front door, roaches scattered across the floor. Of course, I screamed. The doors, cabinets, and woodwork were a speckled brown from roach drippings. I even refused to take my purse in the house for fear that some friendly fellows would climb in and find transportation back to our home, so I locked my purse in the car while I went in to set off bug bombs. All this on the first visit to assess the repairs that needed to be made.

The roaches were only one part of the disaster. There were busted in walls, door facings knocked off the frames, walls brown from nicotine stains, and lint hanging down from the blades of the ceiling fans like moss off a Mississippi oak. Windows were broken and one bedroom was painted with a bright red brick enamel. Perhaps it was the teenager's attempt to escape the awful mess she lived in outside of that room. The stove and oven were coated with an inch of grime that was matted with roaches that had gotten trapped in the grease. What can we say, other than it was a total disaster? There was not much in the house that could be redeemed—the structure maybe, but almost everything else had to be redone and rebuilt at a great cost of time and money to us, since we were the ones blessed with the title to the property.

To say the least, we were devastated. I have a nonprofit and travel a lot so the idea of spending two to three months cleaning toilets, roach droppings, and grease did not appeal to me in the least. And not only that, this house was the last in five that we had to clean and fix to be re-rented over the last five months. We were worn out before we entered the front door. That's when I got the brilliant idea for this book—literally with my head behind the toilet in that dirty house.

I knew we could have avoided that situation if we had just taken action sooner. We would have been much better off to have evicted the renter at the first sign of trouble. I wrote this book to help other landlords know when to spot trouble and avert it as quickly as possible. The fact is Keith and I have something to say and we wanted to say it to anyone who might become a potential landlord.

Looking back at the experience, we could have certainly avoided the problem if we had headed it off at the very beginning. Did we have bad renters? Of course, we did. Yet the situation could only be blamed on us because we saw things from the beginning that should have thrown up red flags all over the field, but we ignored them. We didn't follow our own advice. (Remember, I told you that you would be profiting from our mistakes.)

We were coaxing the monthly rent out of the tenant by visiting him every two weeks and calling him until he would eventually pay. We comforted ourselves by saying, "At least he's paying the rent." What that renter cost us, however, was more money and time than he ever paid out in rent—and that's not taking into account that we had to pay a mortgage payment out of the monthly rent he gave us.

Motivational speaker Brian Tracy gives great advice in his training. One important principle he teaches is that when we look at a disaster or something that is going wrong in our lives we should say, "I am responsible." This was so true in our case with this tenant—we were responsible. We knew the tenant wasn't paying rent on time. But the real signal we should have heeded was the front broken window that he continually promised to repair.

**The Broken Windows Theory**

That broken front window was a huge signal for us to take action. If we had taken care of the window, we would have uncovered the domestic violence issue. Perhaps we could have stopped the abuse if we had inspected the premises on a regular basis and witnessed not only the broken window, but the holes in the walls and the busted door frames – all signs of domestic abuse. Early intervention might have spared the family and us a lot of pain and expense.

Desecration of property usually does not occur overnight. It happens in small increments over time. That is why as landlords we must take care of the little things as they come up and not let them slide until they run down the neighborhood or destroy our property. People who are disrespectful of other people's property will continue their bad behavior until they are stopped. That's why it is better to stop violence at the beginning rather than let it go on until property, neighborhoods and lives are destroyed. It's like an epidemic that starts with one house and then spreads through the family, then the neighborhood.

Malcom Gladwell, award-winning journalist and author, explains in his book *The Tipping Point* the importance of taking care of little things. He says that the Broken Windows theory was the brainchild of James Q. Wilson and George Kelling. Both of these criminologists argued that crime was a result of disorder.[2] If someone in a neighborhood sees a broken window, for instance, he concludes that no one cares about the property. And if the person who owns the property doesn't care and the person who lives in the property doesn't care, then why should he care? Why not break out other windows? Why not vandalize the whole neighborhood? Why not start a crack house next door? After all, no one cares.

Gladwell also makes a case for deterring crime and abuse in any neighborhood. He describes two principles that have proven to be effective to change a neighborhood. One is the "Power of Context,"[3] which states that people raise or lower themselves to the level of their surroundings. In other words, if a person lives continually in a home with broken windows that are taped shut with duct tape (like our renter did), they will eventually become depressed and go to the emotional level that a disheveled home encourages.

The Broken Windows theory prompted the cleanup of New York City and the city's turnaround to become a tourist destination once again. Simply stated the Broken Windows theory says that if broken windows in a

---

[2]Malcolm Gladwell, *The Tipping Point* (New York, NY: Back Bay Books, 2000, 2002), 141.
[3]Malcolm Gladwell, 29.

neighborhood are repaired and the small details taken care of, a whole neighborhood can be turned around from one where crime and drug deals are an everyday occurrence to a neighborhood where people are decent and care about each other. The turnaround is in the details.

The New York Metropolitan Transit Authority (MTA) applied this theory to their subway system back in the 1980s when people were afraid to travel on the subway because of dangerous gang activity. One vigilante had just opened fire on several gang members who had attempted to rob him. Something had to be done to stop the violence. The cure, Wilson and Kelling surmised, was to clean the subway cars of all vestiges of gang emblems and then keep them clean. The MTA began to make sure that no cars went out of the subway station with gang symbols or paintings of any kind written on the outside or inside of the cars.

It would take a gang at least three days of tedious "art work" to get the subway cars painted to their specifications. At that point, the MTA would take the car out of service and repaint it. Gangs became frustrated because they spent days painting the cars, only to have their precious "art work" destroyed by the MTA. The cars were also cleaned regularly and made to look comfortable. By taking care of the little things about the subway car, the whole subway system became safer. People were no longer afraid to ride in them.[4]

---

[4]Malcolm Gladwell, 142–143.

If we take care of the little things, the big things sometimes take care of themselves. The point is watch for small signs of what could become huge problems. Be socially responsible, not just for the neighborhood and because it is the right thing to do, but do it because in the long run it means money in your pocket.

We are convinced that we held a responsibility because we allowed something to continue without our taking a stand. That broken window happened one year into the three-year rental stint we had with that renter. When Keith asked him what happened, he replied, "Oh, that. My son threw a baseball and broke that window. I'll have it fixed next week." We took him at his word and never insisted that he repair the window. Neither did we repair it. Why should we? After all, he said he was going to do it. We let the broken window slide much too long and failed to see it as a warning sign.

It was not until we started cleaning the toilets two years later that the neighbors shared with us about the domestic disturbances that had gone on inside the home. The frequent beatings the wife received had contributed to her suicide. After the wife's death, the husband and his three children vacated the property.

**Honesty in Dealing with Others**

In 1958, Eugene Burdick and William Lederer wrote a book entitled *The Ugly American,* which contained a long laundry list of wrongs that Americans had perpetrated on those in the developing world. While I took issue with a lot of the things that were pointed out, I have to say that the more I see what Americans do to exploit others in the name of money and "the bottom line," the more I understand why we have such a bad reputation in other countries.

We can no longer look the other way when our renters are in need. I'm not saying we should become a charity because we have to make money at this business and I surely know the realities of a renter who continually lies about the rent being in the mail. Yet there are times when we need to have compassion—and that doesn't always mean giving a handout. Sometimes it means helping a renter find a job or perhaps helping out the family at Christmas.

Few governments in the world trust Americans and site greed as the main reason for that dislike. That is why our country is now facing fines for excessive carbon emissions. It is my opinion that the potential fines are not because we are the country that emits the most pollutants—China, India and Poland far exceed us—but because the rest of the world sees us as greedy and overindulgent. We can shrug it off as jealously on their part, and much of it can be attributed to that; but we could have done a lot to prevent that concept from being accepted as the norm if we as individual businesspeople would have been more honest in our dealings with others. Can we start to change that? The very least we can do is to try to think of others.

We would like for our government to be more honest and straightforward, but in reality, they cannot do any better than we do ourselves. If we refuse to tend to the smallest details and deal fairly and with integrity, the government cannot but magnify what is going on at the microcosmic level. The only way to change the big things is to change the small things.

Several years ago I was shocked to see a friend of mine featured on the evening news. Dr. K was a local pediatrician who had too much income and wanted to get into rental property as a way to decrease his tax liability. He owned rentals that he had seriously neglected and the renters had exposed him. I knew him as a kind and compassionate doctor who had built up a huge practice over the years. Then one day soon after the broadcast, he abruptly closed his practice and moved his family out of town. Did it have anything to do with his name appearing on the late night news as a slumlord? We may never know for sure, but it's quite possible that it did.

The news segment on Dr. K was not about his being a great doctor but rather about his neglect as a landlord. Dr. K had purchased several cheap rental houses in a poorer section of town. Each of the rentals had space heaters, no air conditioning, leaking roofs, and an abundance of cockroaches. The houses featured in the exposé had space heaters that were leaking gas and according to the journalist who was interviewing the renters, they had been unable to get the doctor to tend to any repairs and especially to send a technician out to make the space heaters safe.

Of course, Dr. K was unavailable for comment.

Dr. K, just like many professionals, wanted the tax breaks and cash flow from property without realizing that when he bought rentals, he actually started another business—one that would require some of his attention. He failed to realize that he needed to tend to both of his businesses with at least equal compassion toward those whom he treated as a doctor *and* those he rented to as a landlord.

The moral to this story is there are consequences if you do not tend to the details of your rentals and handle your properties responsibly, as well as treat your renters with respect and responsibility. You might even end up on the late night news and have to leave town in a hurry!

Proverbs 29:7 says, "The righteous care about justice for the poor, but the wicked have no such concern." Whether we as landlords have been blessed with one rental house or several, we should be grateful and be good stewards with what we have been entrusted. You may think you are a struggling landlord just barely able to make the monthly mortgages, but according to the rest of the socio-economic world you are blessed. It's a matter of putting it all into perspective.

You may wonder, "What has all this got to do with getting your head from behind a toilet?" Everything. When you have a good attitude about your possessions and about others, it's amazing how your circumstances will change—you will see the light of day and there will be no more cleaning toilets for you!

## Take Care of Business

We wish we lived in a world where no one told a lie or if one did tell a lie his nose would truly grow, but we don't. Renters lie, landlords lie. And I can say that I've seen it equally both ways. If you tell one of your renters that you will have something repaired, you need do what you promised. Either make the repair, call someone to do it, or call the renter and explain why you can't do it right now. Just do what you said you would. We don't like it when our renters lie to us, and they do, so we shouldn't lie to them. I'm a firm believer that we reap what we sow. If you lie, you will get lied to in return.

Now, you may be one of those landlords who never really lies, but you just don't get around to getting repairs done or calling the repairman. Actually, you are doing the same as lying. My point is that truthfulness is a character quality that should be learned pre-kindergarten. Tell the truth and be true to your word. If you say you will do something, do it. Take care of business.

Something else to address is talking badly about your renters behind their backs. We cannot continually talk about someone and expect them to improve the next time. We don't respect those who slander others. The consequences for doing this are enormous. In this business, as well as others (remember we once taught school), it is easy to be cynical and say things that are demeaning and hurtful. Words spoken against someone else are not retrievable. It would be to our benefit to be kind to the poor rather than put them down.

What has all this got to do with being socially responsible? Everything, because being morally responsible is a basic principle of life known as the Golden Rule. It's a rule that is universal to almost all religions and cultures. Jesus said it best, "So in everything, do to others what you would have them do to you, for this sums up the Law and the Prophets" (Matt. 7:12).

Where do you want to be in ten years? Most everything I've heard about encouraging others to look ahead to the next ten years of their lives is in regard to goal setting. Consider this: What if you are old, decrepit, or even dead in ten years? In looking back over your life, what would you like to see that you have accomplished? Have you dealt with people justly? Have you walked in integrity? Have you viewed people as God sees them? All of these are principles that will determine what kind of legacy a person will leave.

You can be the richest person in the world and not be happy. Obviously money helps ease the pain of a lot of injustice, and it certainly helps to be able to get a new car when one needs it; but let's peel away the veneer and ask the question, "How do I really want to be remembered?" Surely it is not as a miserly, bitter person who took advantage of everyone who came across his or her path, but rather a wise, successful, generous businessperson—one who treated people fairly *and* also knew how to handle money.

Jesus said it is better to give than to receive. He did not say this to divest the rich of their wealth nor did Jesus want givers to merely experience the pleasure of giving.

Rather, he wanted to add wealth to the giver because giving increases one's capacity to receive. In order to know how to give, we have to be made aware of the need. A landlord has the ability to be in touch with people's needs and to respond with compassion. Even when struggles occur with tenants, there is usually a compassionate way to handle those difficulties. The hands-on landlord has the advantage to connect with his tenants so that the lease agreement works well for both parties. For this world to change for the better, landlords have to be able to see the struggles of those who may have less than he has and build a bridge of compassion that is sadly lacking in our society today. The United States needs fewer absentee landlords and more compassionate landlords - people like you who want to create wealth and do so in such a way that it will take care of yourself as well as others. Focus on being generous with your God-given gifts.

## Sample Rental Fix-up and Repair Checklist

Address _____

### Entryway

- Sweep/mop floor/wax if necessary
- Clean/paint ceiling/walls/woodwork/baseboards
- Clean/paint closets
- Steam clean carpet
- Replace bulbs/clean light fixtures
- Clean windows
- Clean outlet covers
- Replace electrical outlet covers/broken plug-ins
- Paint front door/replace brass kick plate
- Rekey lock (door and dead bolt)

### Kitchen

- Clean stove top & front
- Clean cabinet shelves & front
- Test dishwasher for leaks/ensure it will run a full cycle
- Clean front of dishwasher
- Check under sink for leaks
- Check faucet for leaks/spraying from the side
- Sweep/mop floor/wax if necessary
- Clean sinks/counter tops
- Caulk around sink/tub walls
- Check for bulbs needing replacement

- Clean drawers
- Clean oven/microwave
- Clean/paint walls/woodwork/baseboards
- Clean light fixtures
- Clean windows/mini blinds
- Clean outlet covers
- Replace electrical outlet covers/broken plug-ins
- Notes:

## Utility Room

- Ensure washer faucets do not drip nor leak under pressure

## Living Room
- Clean/paint ceiling/walls/woodwork/baseboards
- Sweep carpet/clean vinyl floors/entryway
- Steam clean carpet
- Replace bulbs/clean light fixtures/fan blades
- Clean out fireplace/ensure it lights and chimney is clean
- Clean windows/mini blinds—patio doors/vertical blinds
- Clean outlet covers
- Replace electrical outlet covers/broken plug-ins
- Notes:

## Bedroom 1
- Clean/paint ceiling/walls/woodwork/baseboards
- Clean/paint closets

- Steam clean carpet
- Replace bulbs/clean light fixtures/fan blades
- Clean windows/mini-blinds—patio doors/vertical blinds
- Clean outlet covers
- Replace electrical outlet covers/broken plug-ins
- Check doorknob functioning
- Notes:

**Bedroom 2**
- Clean/paint ceiling/walls/woodwork/baseboards
- Clean/paint closets
- Steam clean carpet
- Replace bulbs/clean light fixtures/fan blades
- Clean windows/mini blinds—patio doors/vertical blinds
- Clean outlet covers
- Replace electrical outlet covers/broken plug-ins
- Check doorknob functioning
- Notes:

**Bedroom 3**
- Clean/paint ceiling/walls/woodwork/baseboards
- Clean/paint closets
- Steam clean carpet
- Replace bulbs
- Clean light fixtures/fan blades
- Clean windows/mini blinds—patio doors/vertical blinds
- Clean outlet covers

- Replace electrical outlet covers/broken plug-ins
- Check doorknob functioning
- Notes:

## Bathroom 1
- Replace bulbs/light fixtures
- Caulk around sink/backboards/tub/enclosures/stool
- Clean mirror and light fixture
- Ensure TP holder is tightly fastened to wall
- Ensure towel rack(s) is tightly fastened to wall
- Clean sink/tub/shower
- Shine faucets and shower head
- Check for leaks under sink
- Check water flow from shower head
- Clean and wax vinyl floor
- Sweep carpet/steam clean
- Clean/paint ceiling/walls/woodwork/baseboards
- Replace electrical outlet covers/broken plug-ins
- Check doorknob functioning
- Notes:

## Bathroom 2
- Replace bulbs/light fixtures
- Caulk around sink/backboards/tub/enclosures/stool
- Clean mirror and light fixture
- Ensure TP holder is tightly fastened to wall
- Ensure towel rack(s) is tightly fastened to wall
- Clean sink/tub/shower
- Shine faucets and shower head

- Check for leaks under sink
- Check water flow from shower head
- Clean and wax vinyl floor
- Sweep carpet/steam clean
- Clean/paint ceiling/walls/woodwork/baseboards
- Replace electrical outlet covers/broken plug-ins
- Check doorknob functioning
- Notes:

**Utility Room**
- Check for leaks around faucets and replace/repair as necessary
- Clean/paint ceiling/walls/woodwork/baseboards
- Sweep/clean/wax floors
- Check dryer vent to ensure access to outside
- Replace electrical outlet covers/broken plug-ins
- Check doorknob functioning
- Replace bulbs/light fixtures
- Notes:

**Garage**
- Sweep floor/cleanup
- Vacuum out furnace/hot water closet
- Replace furnace filter
- Test opener to ensure door functioning
- Tighten bolt/nuts on overhead door
- Reset settings for opener remotes
- Rekey side door/deadbolt (same as front door)
- Check fold down ladder for safety
- Remove junk left in attic
- Notes:

**Outside**
- Mow/edge/trim yard
- Clean flower beds
- Clean oil spots from driveway
- Trim trees and bushes
- Repair fences
- Paint house as appropriate
- Repair/replace trim boards
- Repair wooden fence
- Repair/replace mailbox post/mail box
- Repair siding as appropriate
- Caulk around garage door/windows/patio doors
- Notes:

**Exterior**

- Check outside faucets for drips or leaks under pressure

# About the Authors

## Nancy Huff

Nancy has an undergraduate degree in mathematics and a Masters Degree in Teaching English as a Second Language. She has taught in public and private schools.

She runs a nonprofit, Teach the Children International that works with refugee children in crisis.

She has been involved in real estate with Keith for over 37 years, selling real estate, flipping houses, purchasing rentals and maintaining them.

## Keith Huff

After receiving his Masters Degree in applied mathematics, Keith started his professional career at Boeing Airplane Company in Wichita, Kansas as a computer programmer. He later worked for Amoco Petroleum in Denver, Colorado and in Tulsa, Oklahoma as a computer programmer and Help Desk Supervisor. He retired from Amoco in 1999 and started his own real estate company, Global Network Realty.

Keith and Nancy have been married for 39 years and have two adult children and four grandchildren.

Ever since he can remember, Keith has been interested in real estate.

# Global Network Realty

Global Network Realty (GNR) is a real estate company located in Tulsa, Oklahoma. We are dedicated to providing quality dependable service whether you are looking for a home for you and your family, seeking to sell a home, or adding a rental property to your portfolio.

We promote local landlords and are here to serve you by helping you be the best landlord you can be.

Contact Keith if you are looking for a home in the Tulsa, Oklahoma area.

[GNRealtyLLC@aol.com](mailto:GNRealtyLLC@aol.com)
GNRealtyLLC.com

Made in the USA
Charleston, SC
14 May 2014